Name ______________________ Class ______________ Date

Skills Worksheet

Life Skills

AF681073

Being a Wise Consumer

COMPARING MEDICINE PRICES

Anyone who has recently purchased over-the-counter (OTC) drugs knows that they can be very expensive. Learning to be a wise consumer by comparing costs before making a purchase can help you save money.

Two Drug Bottles

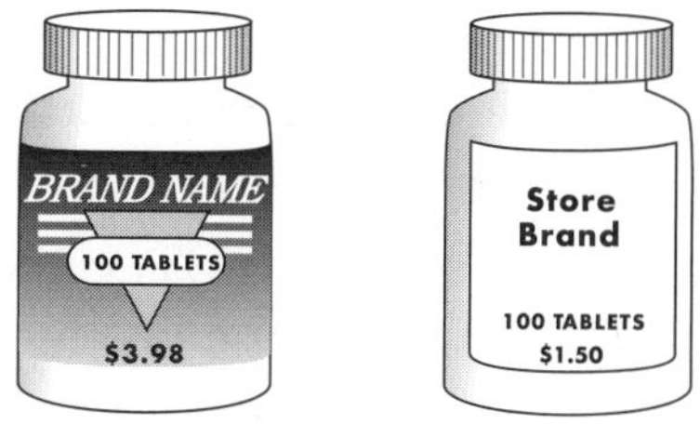

1. Compare and contrast the brand-name packaging with the store-brand packaging. How would you describe the packaging of each drug?

____

____

2. Which kind of packaging has more appeal? Which do you think is easier to recognize? Explain your answers.

____

____

3. Why do you think brand-name manufacturers choose the type of packaging that they do?

____

____

4. Which drug costs less? Why do you think there is a difference in cost?

____

____

5. What is the difference between generic and brand-name drugs?

____

____

6. How can you make sure that the contents of two different brands of a drug are the same or are equally safe and effective?

____

____

Name ______________________ Class ______________ Date ______________

Skills Worksheet

Life Skills

Evaluating Media Messages

COMPARING OVER-THE-COUNTER MEDICINES

Many magazines contain advertisements for over-the-counter (OTC) medicines. Careful review of these ads can help you make good choices about medicines.

1. Skim magazines for OTC medicine ads. For each ad you find, list the magazine source, the product advertised, uses for the product, and the product's active ingredients in the table below.

Magazine	Product	Uses	Active ingredient(s)

2. When choosing an OTC medicine, what are three guidelines one should keep in mind?

____

____

____

3. Select one of the ads. What information does it provide to help you meet the guidelines for safely choosing an OTC medicine?

____

____

____

4. Based on what you know about choosing a safe and effective OTC medicine, would you purchase the medicine described in your selected ad? Why or why not?

____

____

____

Name ______________________ Class ______________ Date ____________

Skills Worksheet

Life Skills

Communicating Effectively

WRITING A PUBLIC SERVICE ANNOUNCEMENT

Public service announcements (PSAs) can help teens learn about the consequences of drug misuse or abuse. They can also help teens learn to use refusal skills. In this activity, you will plan and design a PSA to educate your classmates about the effects of drugs on the brain.

1. Messages about drug use can focus on either the positive or negative consequences of drug misuse or abuse. A positive-consequence message emphasizes the positive outcome of using drugs safely. A negative-consequence message emphasizes the harmful outcomes of drug misuse or abuse. Messages can also focus on refusal strategies by providing different ways teens can resist peer pressure to use drugs in unsafe ways. Which approach(es) will you use in your PSA?

   ____

2. What message about drug use and its effect on the brain do you want to send to your peers?

   ____

3. Think about the different types of media you can use to deliver your PSA. Which type will you use? For example, you could develop a poster, a written ad, or a radio or television script.

   ____

4. In the space below, write a script, draft a print advertisement, or sketch a design for your PSA.

Name ______________________ Class ______________ Date ______________

Skills Worksheet

Life Skills: Express Lesson

Evaluating Media Messages

TRUTH IN ADVERTISING

Dietary supplements and herbal remedies are not regulated by the Food and Drug Administration. Therefore, consumers must be media-savvy in order to evaluate the risks and benefits of these products. Study the following advertisement for a dietary supplement. Then answer the questions.

SuperEnhance 2004

Are you tired and run-down? Is excess weight interfering with your ability to have an active, happy life? Does late-night studying make it impossible to keep your eyes open during the day? SuperEnhance 2004 is just what you've been waiting for! This miraculous blend of all-natural ingredients, used for centuries by Chinese and Native American doctors, can now be your key to a trim, energized, and healthy physique! Just 2 capsules of this revolutionary formula, taken 30–60 minutes before each meal, will set you on the road to long-term health, vitality, and beauty.

Susan L. from Phoenix writes, "I can't believe the difference! I lost 6 pounds the first week! Now I use SuperEnhance 2004 to keep me energized and happy—I have a new sparkle in my eye!"

Bob Q. from Indianapolis writes, "SuperEnhance 2004 was a life-saver for me! My spare tire disappeared, my running times improved, and my hair stopped thinning!"

Ingredients
SuperEnhance 2004
Ephedra Alkaloids
Caffeine
Willow Bark Extract
Chromium picolinate
Cayenne
Ginger

Join the thousands of happy SuperEnhance 2004 customers. Order a 30-day supply of SuperEnhance 2004 now and receive, with your paid purchase, a bonus bottle of 60—a ten-day supply—ABSOLUTELY FREE! Send check or money order to PO Box 2004, Anycity, Illinois. Allow four weeks for processing.

1. What claims are made that should lead you to conclude SuperEnhance 2004 is a fraudulent product?

____

____

____

2. Use library resources or the HealthLinks Web site to learn more about the ingredients in SuperEnhance 2004. What potentially dangerous combinations of substances exist? Which ingredients have little or no value?

____

____

____

Name ______________________ Class ______________ Date ____________

Skills Worksheet

NERVOUS SYSTEM

Life Skills: Express Lesson

Communicating Effectively

WRITING A BROCHURE

Congratulations! You've been hired as the Feel More Travel Agency's newest tour guide. The nervous system is your responsibility, and you need to design a brochure for an adventurous tour of the system. Follow the steps below to help you plan your design.

1. What are the highlights of the tour, must-see destinations, and trendy hot spots?

____

____

____

____

2. What exciting activities take place in your system?

____

____

____

____

____

3. What are the imports and exports of your system?

____

____

____

____

4. Are there any precautions that travelers should take when visiting your system?

____

____

____

5. Be creative. Make your brochure by folding a piece of construction paper into thirds. Write text that emphasizes the highlights of your tour. Illustrate your brochure with drawings, computer graphics, or pictures cut from magazines.

Name ______________________ Class ______________ Date ____________

Life Skills: Express Lesson

Being a Wise Consumer

SELECTING HEALTHCARE PROVIDERS

Because the quality of healthcare varies, it is important to choose your doctor with care. Follow the directions in steps 1 and 2 to practice choosing a doctor who best meets your needs.

1. Add to the checklist additional criteria that you want your doctor to meet.

______ My doctor must be board-certified.

______ My doctor must be allowed to treat people at my preferred hospital.

______ My doctor must have a contract with my health insurance plan.

______ My doctor must have after-school and weekend hours.

______ ____

______ ____

______ ____

2. Research doctors in your community using library resources. Search for doctors in your area who practice pediatrics. List three pediatricians in the table below. Find out about his or her education, licensure, certification, and hospital affiliations. You should also find out their insurance affiliations and the doctors' office hours. Use these resources to fill out the table, making sure to find the answers to the special concerns you listed in Step 1. Highlight the physicians who meet your criteria.

Doctor's name	Board-certified in pediatrics	Affiliations with my local hospital	Participant in my health insurance plan	After-school and weekend hours

Life Skills: Express Lesson

Being a Wise Consumer

COMPARING HEALTH INSURANCE PLANS

PART I

Choosing the right type of health insurance plan can be tricky. In the table below, record the features of each type of insurance plan.

Health insurance plan	Description	Benefits	Drawbacks
HMO			
PPO			

PART II

Use library resources to find information on an HMO or PPO that offers services in your area. Then answer the following questions.

1. Are the doctors under contract to the plan near where you live? Would you be able to easily access healthcare if you were to enroll in the plan?

____

____

2. Does the plan require that you choose a primary care provider from a list? What information does the insurance company provide to help you make an informed decision when choosing a doctor?

____

____

____

3. If you go outside the plan for care, how much do you have to pay? Are there exceptions for emergencies?

____

____

____

Name ______________________ Class ______________ Date ______________

Skills Worksheet

Reteaching

Section: Drugs

PART I

Complete the network tree about over-the-counter (OTC) drugs by using the terms from the list below. Some terms are used more than once, others are not used at all.

acetaminophen	relieves pain
temazepam	causes sleepiness
increases alertness	methylphenidate
antacids	focuses attention in ADHD

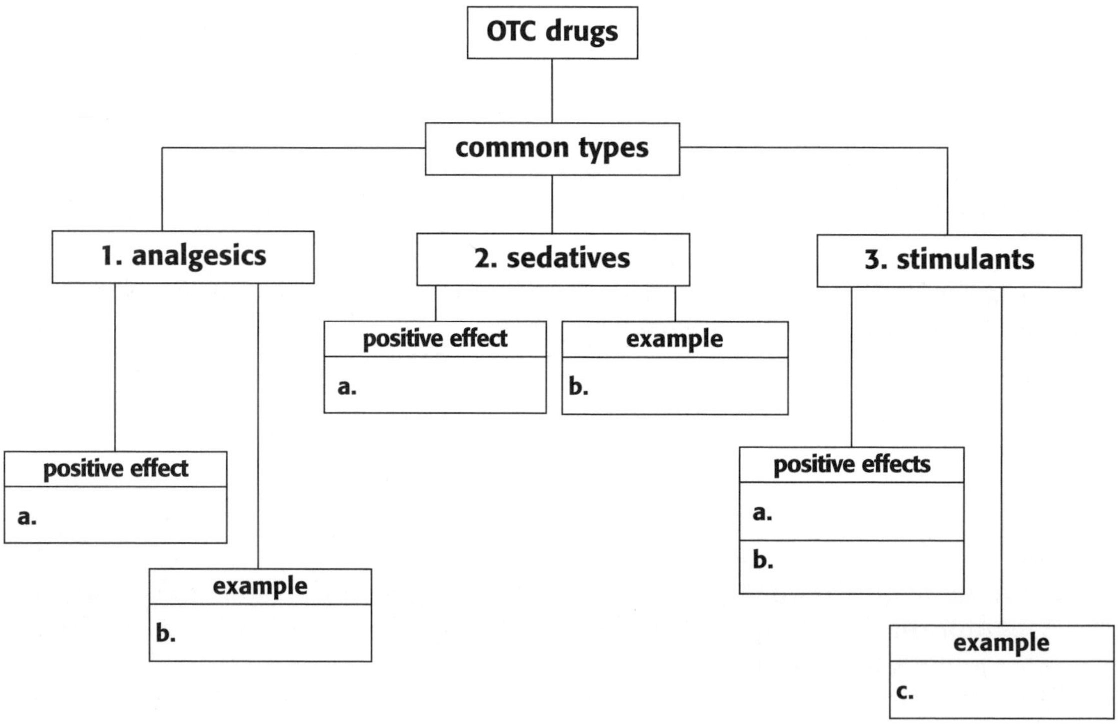

PART II

Answer the following questions in the spaces provided.

4. What are the two qualities that a medicine must possess?

____

____

5. What distinguishes medicines from drugs of abuse?

____

____

Name ______________ Class ______________ Date ______________

Skills Worksheet

Reteaching

Section: Drugs as Medicines

Study the package from an over-the-counter (OTC) medicine. Then answer the questions in the spaces provided.

Active ingredient (in each tablet): Acetaminophen 500 mg . . . . **Purposes:** Pain reliever/fever reducer

Uses (for the temporary relief of):
- headache
- backache
- muscular aches
- toothache
- aches from common cold
- menstrual cramps
- arthritis pain
- fever

Warnings:

Alcohol warning: If you consume 3 or more alcoholic drinks every day, ask your doctor whether you should take acetaminophen or other pain relievers/fever reducers. Acetaminophen may cause liver damage.

Do not use:
- with any other product containing acetaminophen
- for more than 10 days for pain unless directed by a doctor
- for more than 3 days for fever unless directed by a doctor

Stop using and ask a doctor if:
- symptoms do not improve
- new symptoms occur
- pain or fever persists or gets worse
- redness or swelling is present

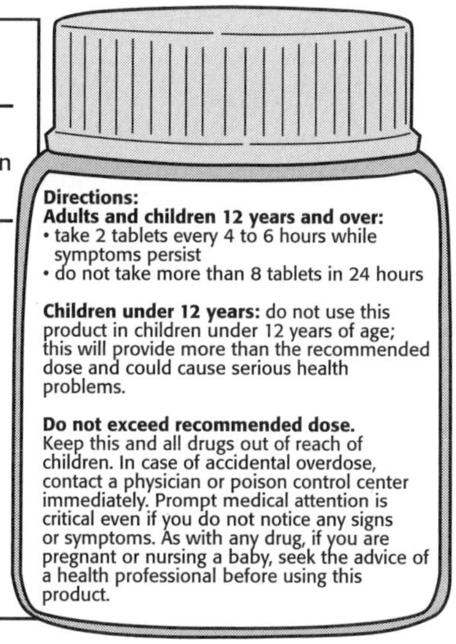

1. What is the active ingredient in this OTC medication?

____

2. What symptoms does this medication treat?

____

____

____

3. Read the directions. What would be your correct dose? How often would you take this medication?

____

____

4. What are the possible side effects of this medication?

____

____

____

____

Name ______________________ Class ______________ Date ______________

Skills Worksheet

Reteaching

Section: Drugs and the Brain

PART I

Fill in the missing word or phrase in each of the following sentences.

1. A person who is ______________________ to a drug is physically dependent on that drug.

2. Resisting pressure to abuse drugs is a responsible ______________________.

3. The first step in the addiction process is ______________________.

4. A(n) ______________________ drug affects a person's mood or behavior.

5. The body's reaction when it doesn't receive a drug it depends on is

______________________.

6. If a person requires higher and higher dosages of a drug to produce the same effects, that person has developed a(n) ______________________ to the drug.

7. When a person's body comes to expect the presence of a drug,

______________________ dependence, or addiction occurs.

8. Although legal for adults, ______________________ and nicotine are addictive drugs.

PART II

Unscramble each behavioral warning sign of addiction.

9. SSLO FO TEISETNR NI OHSOWKOCLR

_ _ _ _ / _ _ / _ _ _ _ _ _ _ _ / _ _ / _ _ _ _ _ _ _ _ _ _

10. TDCAIRAM CEANHG FO CAAPEANPRE

_ _ _ _ _ _ _ _ / _ _ _ _ _ _ / _ _ / _ _ _ _ _ _ _ _ _ _

11. NEHCGA FO FRDEINS

_ _ _ _ _ _ / _ _ / _ _ _ _ _ _ _

12. NANDIUELPXE ODOM NWGISS

_ _ _ _ _ _ _ _ _ _ _ / _ _ _ _ / _ _ _ _ _ _

Name ______________________________ Class ______________ Date ____________

Skills Worksheet

Concept Review

Section: Drugs

PART I

Write the letter of the correct answer on the line.

______ **1.** A written order from a doctor for a specific medicine is called a(n)
- **a.** prescription.
- **b.** drug.
- **c.** side effect.
- **d.** antibiotic.

______ **2.** The two origins of all drugs are
- **a.** hospitals and pharmacies.
- **b.** drug stores and doctors' offices.
- **c.** natural sources and laboratories.
- **d.** pharmacies and grocery stores.

______ **3.** A method of drug delivery in which the drug is applied directly to certain areas of the body and absorbed into the skin is called
- **a.** a transdermal patch.
- **b.** an implanted pump.
- **c.** inhalation therapy.
- **d.** topical application.

PART II

Answer each question in the space provided.

4. What are the three qualities that make a drug useful as a medicine?

____

____

5. What is the distinction between a drug and a medicine?

____

____

6. How do drugs of abuse differ from medicines?

____

____

Name ______________________ Class ______________ Date ____________

Skills Worksheet

Concept Review

Section: Drugs as Medicines

PART I

Answer the following questions in the space provided.

1. What are two reasons that prescriptions are required for some medicines?

____

____

2. What information does a prescription include?

____

____

3. What are the steps in the approval process for a new medicine?

____

____

PART II

Write the letter of the correct answer in the blank.

______ **4.** Which of the following is a term used to describe a drug or medicine that affects the brain?

a. generic
b. prescription
c. psychoactive
d. over-the-counter (OTC)

______ **5.** How do herbal remedies differ from OTC medicines?

a. Herbal remedies are not effective.
b. Herbal remedies are not safe.
c. Herbal remedies have serious side effects.
d. Herbal remedies are not FDA regulated.

______ **6.** Possible symptoms of anaphylactic shock include

a. itching all over the body.
b. swelling in the mouth or throat.
c. difficulty breathing and a pounding heart.
d. All of the above

______ **7.** Taking any combination of alcohol, sedatives, or tranquilizers can cause

a. increased drowsiness and coordination loss.
b. agitation and accidents.
c. fever and chills.
d. headache and difficulty sleeping.

Name ______________________________ Class ______________ Date ____________

Skills Worksheet

Concept Review

Section: Drugs and the Brain

PART I

Complete each of the following statements with the correct word or phrase.

1. The uncomfortable physical and psychological symptoms produced when a physically dependent user stops using drugs is called ______________________.

2. Chemicals that influence the way that neurons communicate with each other are called ______________________.

3. The condition in which a person's body relies on a given drug in order to function is ______________________.

4. A condition in which a person can no longer control his or her drug use is called ______________________.

5. When a person's body forms a(n) ______________________ to a regularly abused drug, higher and higher doses are needed to produce the same effects.

PART II

Write the letter of the correct answer in the blank.

______ **6.** Which sequence describes the path to drug addiction?
- **a.** drug use, tolerance, dependence, addiction
- **b.** drug use, dependence, tolerance, addiction
- **c.** drug use, addiction, dependence, tolerance
- **d.** tolerance, drug use, dependence, addiction

______ **7.** The best way to avoid addiction is to
- **a.** research treatment options.
- **b.** avoid misusing or abusing drugs.
- **c.** enroll in a treatment program.
- **d.** only experiment with drugs.

______ **8.** Behavioral warning signs of addiction include
- **a.** loss of interest in schoolwork and change of appearance.
- **b.** change of friends and unexplained mood swings.
- **c.** absence from school and unexplained need for money.
- **d.** All of the above

______ **9.** The neurotransmitter responsible for producing pleasure is
- **a.** serotonin.
- **b.** epinephrine.
- **c.** dopamine.
- **d.** None of the above

Name ______________________ Class ______________ Date ____________

Assessment

Quiz

Section: Drugs

Write the letter of the correct definition on the line.

a. any substance that causes a change in a person's physical or psychological state

b. any medicine that can be bought without a prescription

c. a written order from a doctor for a specific medicine

d. any drug used to cure, prevent, or treat illness or discomfort

e. any effect that is caused by a drug and that is different from the drug's intended effect

______ **1.** medicine

______ **2.** drug

______ **3.** side effect

______ **4.** over-the-counter (OTC) medicine

______ **5.** prescription

Name ______________________ Class ______________ Date ____________

Assessment

Quiz

Section: Drugs as Medicines

PART I

Match each definition with the correct term.

a. a drug or medicine that affects thought, perception, or feelings

b. when a drug reacts with another drug, food, or dietary supplement to make the effect of one of the drugs either greater or smaller

c. a medicine made by a company other than the company that developed the original medicine

______ **1.** generic medicine

______ **2.** drug interaction

______ **3.** psychoactive drug

PART II

Write the letter of the correct answer in each blank.

______ **4.** The chemical component that gives a medicine its action is called its
- **a.** clinical trial.
- **b.** generic equivalent.
- **c.** active ingredient.
- **d.** supplement.

______ **5.** A complete prescription includes all of the following information *except*
- **a.** the amount of medicine to take.
- **b.** the expiration date of the medicine.
- **c.** how often you should take the medicine.
- **d.** the time you should take the medicine.

Name ______________________ Class ____________ Date ____________

Assessment

Quiz

Section: Drugs and the Brain

Write the letter of the correct answer in each blank.

______ **1.** Which of the following statements describes how drugs can change the way neurons communicate with each other?
a. Drugs can act like neurotransmitters.
b. Drugs can block neurotransmitters.
c. Drugs can change the amount of neurotransmitters in a synapse.
d. all of the above

______ **2.** A condition in which a user needs more of a drug to get the same effect is called
a. addiction.
b. drug tolerance.
c. physical dependence.
d. withdrawal.

______ **3.** Drugs of abuse include
a. marijuana.
b. cocaine.
c. nicotine.
d. All of the above

______ **4.** The path to drug addiction includes the following steps: dependence, tolerance, addiction, and drug use. What is the correct sequence of these steps?
a. 4, 2, 1, 3
b. 2, 4, 3, 1
c. 3, 1, 4, 2
d. 4, 3, 2, 1

______ **5.** Which of the following statements does *not* accurately describe addiction?
a. It is not treatable.
b. It involves a physical and psychological need for a drug.
c. It is a condition in which a user can no longer control his or her drug use.
d. It is a treatable disease.

Name ______________________ Class ______________ Date ____________

Assessment

Chapter Test

Understanding Drugs and Medicines

PART I

Match the terms on the left with the definitions on the right.

_____ **1.** analgesic

_____ **2.** stimulant

_____ **3.** vaccine

_____ **4.** over-the-counter (OTC) medicine

_____ **5.** prescription medicine

_____ **6.** sedative

_____ **7.** addiction

_____ **8.** active ingredient

a. a drug that requires a written order from a doctor because it treats serious health conditions or is a very powerful medicine

b. a medicine available without a prescription

c. a medicine that relieves pain

d. a drug that increases alertness

e. a chemical that gives a drug its action

f. a medicine that prevents infection in people exposed to infectious agents

g. a condition in which a person cannot control his or her drug use

h. a medicine that causes sleepiness

PART II

Write the letter of the correct answer in each blank.

_____ **9.** How do drugs of abuse differ from medicines?

a. Drugs of abuse have no medical purpose, while medicines treat, prevent, or cure illness.
b. Medicines have no medical purpose, while drugs of abuse treat, prevent, or cure illness.
c. Drugs of abuse are psychoactive, while medicines are not.
d. Drugs of abuse always cause addiction, while medicines never do.

_____ **10.** Possible problems with medicines include

a. allergic reactions.
b. anaphylactic shock.
c. side effects.
d. All of the above

______**11.** Which sequence accurately describes the testing of medicines for safety?
a. tests on cell cultures, tests on animals, clinical trials, tests on healthy humans
b. tests on cell cultures, tests on animals, tests on healthy humans, clinical trials
c. clinical trials, tests on cell cultures, tests on animals, tests on healthy humans
d. tests on cell cultures, clinical trials, tests on animals, tests on healthy humans

______**12.** While playing soccer, Steve sprained his ankle. His doctor has prescribed an anti-inflammatory medicine. Before taking the new medicine, Steve should
a. ask the doctor if he can take a generic form of the medicine.
b. ask the doctor if there are any side effects.
c. ask the doctor what to do if side effects occur.
d. All of the above

______**13.** Chemical messengers that help the brain process information and affect emotions are released at
a. neurotransmitters.
b. synapses.
c. tiny spaces.
d. neurons.

______**14.** In order to be useful as a medicine, a drug must
a. be safe.
b. be effective.
c. have only minor side effects.
d. All of the above

______**15.** What are the two origins of all drugs?
a. pharmacies and doctor's offices
b. doctor's offices and grocery stores
c. natural sources and laboratories
d. laboratories and pharmacies

______**16.** When choosing an OTC medicine, you should always
a. decide what kind of OTC medicine will work best for you.
b. read the list of uses to find out if the medicine will relieve your illness.
c. decide whether you want a generic or brand-name medicine.
d. All of the above

______ **17.** Methods used to administer medicines include
a. implanted pumps and inhalation.
b. injection and ingestion.
c. transdermal patches and topical application.
d. All of the above

______ **18.** The best way to avoid addiction is to
a. avoid drugs.
b. enroll in a drug treatment program.
c. choose friends who use drugs.
d. only occasionally experiment.

______ **19.** Drug withdrawal keeps an addiction going because
a. the addict loses control of his or her behavior.
b. the unpleasant symptoms drive the addict to take more of the drug to relieve the symptoms.
c. drug use activates the brain reward system.
d. laboratories and pharmacies have drugs.

______ **20.** Experimentation with drugs can lead to addiction because
a. experimentation can lead to a more regular pattern of abuse.
b. pleasure can lead to repeated use, resulting in tolerance and then physical dependence.
c. adolescent brains are more vulnerable to the effects of drugs than adult brains are.
d. All of the above

Name ______________________ Class ______________ Date ______________

Assessment

Chapter Test

Understanding Drugs and Medicine

PART I

Match the terms on the right with the descriptions on the left.

______ **1.** qualities that make a drug useful as a medicine

______ **2.** methods of delivering drugs to the body

______ **3.** origins of all drugs

______ **4.** drugs taken for mind-altering effects, but which have no medical purpose

a. safety, effectiveness, minor side effects

b. natural sources and laboratories

c. implanted pump, inhalation, injection, transdermal patch, ingestion, topical application

d. drugs of abuse

PART II

Write the letter of the correct answer on the line.

______ **5.** A condition in which a person uses more of a drug in order to get the same effect is

a. addiction.
b. drug tolerance.
c. physical dependence.
d. withdrawal.

______ **6.** Wise use of medicine involves

a. asking questions, learning about the medicine, and listening to your body.
b. taking medicines that are prescribed for someone else.
c. stopping taking the medicine as soon as you feel better.
d. mixing medicines to see results sooner.

______ **7.** What is the sequence of events in which drugs are approved for medical use?

a. tests on animals, tests on cell cultures, tests on healthy humans, clinical trials
b. tests on cell cultures, tests on animals, clinical trials, tests on healthy humans
c. tests on cell cultures, tests on animals, tests on healthy humans, clinical trials
d. tests on animals, tests on healthy humans, tests on cell cultures, clinical trials

______ **8.** David is suffering from a stuffy nose. In choosing an OTC medication, David should
a. read the list of uses to make sure the medication he chooses will treat his stuffy nose.
b. decide what kind of OTC medication will work best to relieve his symptoms.
c. decide whether he wants a generic or a brand-name medication.
d. All of the above

______ **9.** Prescriptions are required for some medicines because
a. most people are not smart enough to choose their own medicines.
b. some diseases are very serious and some drugs are very powerful.
c. no one would go to the doctor if all medicines were available OTC.
d. OTC medicines are more expensive.

______ **10.** Sharon's doctor prescribed an antibiotic for her ear infection. Shortly after she took the medicine, she noticed her skin itching and felt tightness in her chest. These symptoms
a. indicate that Sharon is having a serious reaction to her medication.
b. require emergency medical assistance.
c. indicate that Sharon may be experiencing an anaphylactic reaction to her antibiotic.
d. All of the above

PART III

Match the drugs on the left with their effects on the right.

______ **11.** analgesic
______ **12.** antihistamine
______ **13.** bronchodilator
______ **14.** steroid anti-inflammatory
______ **15.** stimulant
______ **16.** antianxiety medicine
______ **17.** vaccine
______ **18.** sedative
______ **19.** antacid

a. reduces inflammation of the skin
b. helps people who are panicked calm down
c. causes sleepiness
d. opens airways
e. increases alertness
f. relieves pain
g. prevents infections in people exposed to infectious agents
h. neutralizes stomach acid to relieve heartburn
i. relieves allergy symptoms

PART IV

Answer the following question in the space provided.

20. Drugs affect the way the brain works. Some drugs change how messages in the brain are sent and activate the brain reward system. When this happens, a predictable course of events occurs that results in addiction. Describe how drugs of abuse affect the brain, leading to addiction. What are the effects of addiction? How can addiction be avoided?

Name ______________________ Class ______________ Date ____________

Assessment

Alternative Assessment

Choose one of the following topics:

a. the misuse and abuse of drugs

b. types of over-the-counter (OTC) drugs and their uses

c. the effects of common types of drugs

d. appropriate uses of medicines

Prepare a multimedia presentation to inform an audience of your peers about one of these topics. In other words, use multiple types of media, such as a slide show and a recorded presentation, to deliver your message. Summarize your presentation in the space below.

Name ____________________ Class ______________ Date ____________

Assessment

Standardized Test Practice

Read the following passage and answer questions 1 through 3.

Any drug that is used to cure, prevent, or treat illness or discomfort is called a medicine. Among the most common medicines are analgesics, antihistamines, and antacids. Some of these medicines require a prescription while over-the-counter medicines do not require a prescription. A prescription is a written order from a doctor for a specific medicine. Over-the-counter medicines are medicines that can be bought without a prescription.

Analgesics are medicines that relieve pain. Three common types of over-the-counter analgesics are aspirin, acetaminophen, and ibuprofen. However, some very powerful analgesics may be bought only with a prescription. Examples of such analgesics are the opiates codeine and morphine. Antihistamines are medicines that block the action of the body chemical histamine, which can cause the symptoms of allergic reactions. Antacids are medicines that work against stomach acid, which can cause heartburn.

Test-Taking Tip

An analogy links two pairs of items that share a common relationship. If asked to complete an analogy, focus on the pair provided. Identify the relationship that exists between the items, such as part to whole or category to member. Then find an answer choice that has the same relationship with the third term provided.

______ **1.** Complete the analogy: Over-the-counter is to ibuprofen as prescription is to

A aspirin.
B analgesic.
C acetaminophen.
D codeine.

______ **2.** Antihistamines are to the symptoms of allergic reactions as antacids are to

A heartburn.
B pain.
C aspirin.
D histamine.

3. **Writing Skill** You tell a friend that you have a terrible headache. He suggests that you take one of his prescription painkillers. Describe what you would do. Provide reasons for your actions.

____

____

____

____

____

____

Read the following passage and answer questions 4 through 6.

In the early part of the twentieth century, the U.S. government started to pass laws to help ensure that drugs were safe to use. In 1906, a government agency called the Food and Drug Administration (FDA) was created to control the safety of food, drugs, and cosmetics.

The FDA has developed a process for companies that want to sell a drug in the United States. This process is needed to make sure the drug is safe and effective. After scientists develop or discover a new drug, they test it. Initial testing takes place in laboratories and may include chemical tests or tests on cell cultures. After the initial tests are completed, all drugs are tested on animals to be sure they work.

If the animal testing shows that a drug is safe, then testing for safety may begin on healthy human volunteers. If the drug passes these first tests on humans, the drug is then tested on humans who have the illness that the drug is meant to treat. These larger tests are called clinical trials. During clinical trials, the new drug is compared to existing drugs to see if it is safe and effective. If the clinical trials are successful, then the drug company can apply to the FDA for approval of the drug. The FDA then approves or rejects the drug for sale to the public.

______ **4. Reading Skill** Before a drug becomes available for use by the public, it must be

A studied by physicians.
B approved by the FDA.
C tested on sick animals.
D Both A and B

______ **5. Reading Skill** During clinical trials, a new drug is

A given to humans who have the illness it is meant to treat.
B compared to existing drugs to see if it is safe and effective.
C tested in laboratories.
D Both A and B

6. Writing Skill Describe the sequence of steps that occur from the time a new drug is discovered until it is available for sale to the public.

____

____

____

____

____

____

Read the following passage and answer questions 7 through 9.

Drugs that are not medicines, such as cocaine, nicotine, alcohol, and marijuana, change the way the brain works in ways that are not healthy. These drugs interrupt the balance between the many neurotransmitters needed for normal brain functioning. They affect our judgement in ways that affect our ability to understand and deal with reality. If drugs like these are taken over a long period of time, they can create the powerful changes in feelings and behavior that lead to addiction. Addiction is a condition in which a person can no longer control his or her drug use. When a person becomes addicted to a drug, he or she has developed a physical need for the drug and can't function without it.

______ 7. **Reading Skill** Drugs such as alcohol and marijuana affect the user's judgement by

A making the person feel as if his or her life is out of control.
B causing the person to become physically ill.
C interrupting the balance between neurotransmitters in the person's brain.
D Both A and B

______ 8. **Reading Skill** A person who is addicted to nicotine

A cannot function without it.
B has a physical need for the drug.
C cannot deal with reality.
D Both A and B

9. **Writing Skill** You know that a good friend of yours drinks regularly. You are concerned about the effect her drinking is having on her health and her ability to make wise decisions. Would you share your concerns with your friend? Explain why or why not.

____

____

____

____

____

____

____

____

____

Name ______________________ Class ______________ Date ____________

Use the graph to answer questions 10 through 12.

Misuse of Prescription Drugs in the U.S.

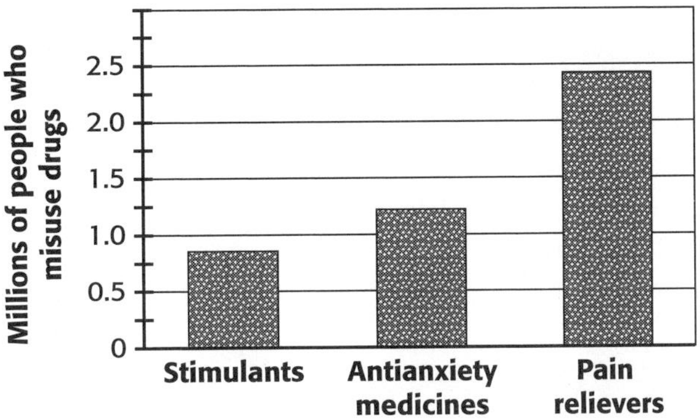

Source: National Household Survey on Drug Abuse.

______ **10.** **Math Skill** About how many more people in the U.S. misuse prescription antianxiety medications than stimulants?

A about 0.5 million
B about 1.0 million
C about 1.5 million
D about 5.0 million

______ **11.** **Math Skill** What ratio compares the number of people who misuse stimulants to the number of people who misuse pain relievers?

A 1 : 3
B 1 : 5
C 2 : 5
D 3 : 1

12. **Writing Skill** A family member is angry that the pharmacist will not refill a prescription pain reliever without a doctor's approval. He claims that the pharmacist is just "too lazy to do his job." Do you agree? Explain why or why not.

Name ______________________ Class ______________ Date ______________

Activity

Datasheet for In-Text Activity

Analyzing Data: Reading a Prescription Label

PHARM STORE Ph. (555) 520-1302

12611 Sahara Ave., Las Vegas, NV 89109

1 **Zola Cobb**
9515 Decatur Blvd., Las Vegas, NV 89110

2 **Rx# 6842571**
Orig Rx date 10/03/04
Date filled 11/13/04

3 **Take 1 Tablet 3 times a day**

4 Qty: **90 TABS**
BACLOFEN 10 MG TABS
DR. F. RANDALL

5 MAY CAUSE DROWSINESS.
ALCOHOL MAY INTENSIFY THIS EFFECT.
USE CARE WHEN OPERATING A CAR
OR DANGEROUS MACHINERY.

6 Two refills remain.
Refill authorization expires on 02/22/05.

1 Patient's name and address

2 Prescription number and dates prescription was filled

3 Instructions for taking medicine

4 Quantity of medicine provided, name and strength of medicine, and doctor's name

5 Side-effect warnings

6 Refill information and expiration date

YOUR TURN

1. How often should this patient take her medicine?

____

2. When the patient finishes the medicine, will she be able to get a refill?

____

3. What is a possible side effect of this medicine?

____

4. How many days will it take for the person to finish the medicine provided?

____

5. **Critical Thinking** Do you think it's safe for this person to stop taking this medicine once she begins to feel better?

____

____

Name ______________________ Class ______________ Date ____________

Activity

Datasheet for In-Text Activity

Making GREAT Decisions

You and Dave used to spend a lot of time together shooting hoops and surfing the Internet. But for the last few months, Dave has been hanging out with a new group. He used to really care about how he looks, but now he looks terrible. Today he asked you for the third time if he could borrow $10. When you told him he hadn't paid you back from the last time, he stormed off and warned you to stay away from him. You suspect that Dave is using drugs.

Write down how you would ask your friend if he has a drug problem. Remember to use the decision-making steps.

Give thought to the problem.
Review your choices.
Evaluate the consequences of each choice.
Assess and choose the best choice.
Think it over afterward.

Name ____________________ Class ____________ Date ____________

Activity

Decision-Making Activity

Reasons for Use of Legal Drugs

Work in small groups. Present your group's list to the class. Remember to use the decision-making steps: Give thought to the problem, Review your choices, Evaluate the consequences of each choice, Assess and choose the best choice, and Think it over afterward.

1. Brainstorm to make a list of situations in which using an over-the-counter (OTC) drug is appropriate.
2. Make a list of the common OTC drugs used on such occasions.
3. Develop a set of guidelines for using OTC medicines. Be certain to include what a person should do to avoid prolonged or repeated use of an OTC medicine.
4. Present your guidelines to the class.

Name ______________________ Class ______________ Date ____________

Activity

Decision-Making Activity

Using Legal Drugs Safely

Work in small groups. Present your group's work to the class. Remember to use the decision-making steps: Give thought to the problem, Review your choices, Evaluate the consequences of each choice, Assess and choose the best choice, and Think it over afterward.

1. Choose one of the following guidelines for using legal drugs:

a. Don't mix medications without checking with a physician or a pharmacist.

b. If you have ever had an allergic reaction to a drug or food, make sure you tell a physician before you use any medication.

c. Don't use over-the-counter drugs for a long period of time.

d. Don't think that if a little bit of a drug makes you feel good, then more will make you feel better.

e. Don't take a prescription medication unless it was prescribed for you. Don't use a medication prescribed for someone else, even if you seem to have the same problem.

f. Ask the pharmacist to tell you about the drug's purpose, its side effects, and its interactions with food and other drugs, as well as the dosage and length of time you should take the drug.

g. Keep all drugs away from children.

2. As a group, write a public service announcement for your guideline. Your announcement should state the guideline and explain why it is important.

____

____

____

____

____

____

____

____

3. Present your public service announcement to the class.

Lesson Plan

Section: Drugs

Pacing

1 block = 45 minutes

Regular Schedule	**with lab(s):** N/A	**without lab(s):** 1 day
Block Schedule	**with lab(s):** N/A	**without lab(s):** 0.5 day

Objectives

1. List three qualities that make a drug useful as a medicine.
2. Name the two sources of all drugs.
3. Identify four different types of medicines and their effects on the body.
4. Identify five different ways that drugs can enter the body.
5. Describe why some drugs are considered drugs of abuse.

National Health Education Standards Covered

1.1 Analyze how behavior can impact health maintenance and disease prevention.

2.6 Analyze situations requiring professional health services.

4.3 Evaluate the impact of technology on personal, family, and community health.

7.2 Express information and opinions about health issues.

KEY
SE = Student Edition
TE = Teacher Edition
CRF = Chapter Resource File

Block 1

FOCUS *10 minutes*

- ❑ **What's Your Health IQ?** To assess student knowledge about drugs and medicines, have students take the pretest on their health IQ. Answers can be found in the TE.
- ❑ **Bellringer** TE. Ask students to name four medicines they have heard of and what each medicine is used for. **(Basic)**

MOTIVATE *5 minutes*

- ❑ **Activity** TE. Have students develop definitions for "prevention," "cure," and "relief" and think of medications that fit in each category. **(General)**

TEACH *20 minutes*

- ❑ **Identifying Misconceptions** TE. Tell students that taking a double dose of a medicine after forgetting to take the medicine can lead to serious side-effects or overdose.

- ❑ **Teaching Transparency** Types of Medicines. Use this graphic to inform students about the various types of medicines.
- ❑ **Using the Table** Table 1, TE. Have students compare various aspects of the table. **(Advanced)**
- ❑ **Group Activity** Developing a New Medicine, TE. Have students work in small groups to write and perform advertisements for a new medicine. **(General)**
- ❑ **Teaching Tip** Drugs of Abuse, TE. Have students research drugs of abuse using library resources and write a report to summarize their findings. **(Advanced)**
- ❑ **Biology Connection** America's Most Popular Drug, TE. Tell students about caffeine, the most widely consumed drug in the country, and its addictive effects. **(Basic)**
- ❑ **Using the Figure** Figure 2, TE. Have students consider the delivery methods of specific drugs. Have them give examples of drugs that enter the body in the ways shown in the figure. **(General)**

CLOSE *10 minutes*

- ❑ **Concept Review Worksheet** Section 1, CRF. This exercise reinforces the material covered in the section. **(General)**
- ❑ **Section Quiz** Section 1, CRF. Students answer five questions that review the section content. **(General)**

HOMEWORK *30 minutes*

- ❑ **Life Skills Worksheet** Comparing Medicine Prices, CRF. Students compare costs of over-the-counter drugs. **(General)**
- ❑ **Decision-Making Activity** Reasons for Use of Legal Drugs, CRF. Students develop a set of guidelines for using over-the-counter drugs. **(General)**
- ❑ **Parent Discussion Guide** Parent Letter and Survey, CRF. Send home with students the Parent Letter and Parent Survey for this chapter.
- ❑ **Section Review** Section 1, SE. Assign questions 1–9 for review, homework, or as a quiz.

OTHER RESOURCE OPTIONS

- ❑ **Reteaching Worksheet** Section 1, CRF. Students complete this worksheet to reinforce the ideas of the section. **(Basic)**
- ❑ **Expanding the Table** Table 1, TE. Have each student research one type of medicine in the table and create a chart summarizing aspects of the medicine. **(General)**
- ❑ **Skill Builder** Interpreting Visuals, TE. Have students compare television or magazine advertisements for similar medicines and report on their conclusions. **(General)**

- ❑ **Current Health** Articles and activities related to the chapter topics may be found at **go.hrw.com.** Type in keyword **HH4 CH09T.**
- ❑ **Video Select** Videos related to the chapter topics may be found at **go.hrw.com.** Type in keyword **HD4 MEDV.**
- ❑ **Internet Connect** Antibiotics, HealthLinks code: HH4013. Students use Internet sources to research antibiotics and their uses.
- ❑ **Guided Reading Audio CD Program** Understanding Drugs and Medicines Script. Assign Section 1. The audio program is a reading of the chapter content for ELL students, auditory learners, and struggling readers.

Lesson Plan

Section: Drugs as Medicines

Pacing

1 block = 45 minutes

Regular Schedule	**with lab(s):** N/A	**without lab(s):** 1 day
Block Schedule	**with lab(s):** N/A	**without lab(s):** 0.5 day

Objectives

1. Describe the process by which drugs are approved for medical use.
2. State two reasons why prescriptions are required for some medicines.
3. State two factors to consider when choosing over-the-counter (OTC) medicines.
4. Describe three problems that can occur when taking some medicines.
5. List six things you should do to be able to use medicines wisely.

National Health Education Standards Covered

1.1 Analyze how behavior can impact health maintenance and disease prevention.

1.3 Explain the impact of personal health behaviors on the functioning of body systems.

1.6 Describe how to delay onset and reduce risks of potential health problems during adulthood.

1.7 Analyze how public health policies and government regulations influence health promotion and disease prevention.

2.1 Evaluate the validity of health information, products, and services.

2.6 Analyze situations requiring professional health services.

3.1 Analyze the role of individual responsibility for enhancing health.

3.3 Analyze the short-term and long-term consequences of safe, risky, and harmful behaviors.

5.1 Demonstrate skills for communicating effectively with family, peers, and others.

6.3 Predict immediate and long-term impact of health decisions on the individual, family, and community.

7.2 Express information and opinions about health issues.

7.4 Demonstrate the ability to influence and support others in making positive health choices.

KEY
SE = Student Edition
TE = Teacher Edition
CRF = Chapter Resource File

Block 2

FOCUS *5 minutes*

- ❑ **Bellringer** TE. Have students write down reasons that prescription and OTC medicines have instructions and precautions written on their packaging. **(BASIC)**

MOTIVATE *5 minutes*

- ❑ **Demonstration** TE. Students evaluate information on OTC products. **(GENERAL)**

TEACH *25 minutes*

- ❑ **Group Activity** OTC Posters, TE. Have groups of students create poster collages of OTC medicine advertisements they have found. **(BASIC)**
- ❑ **Using the Figure** Figure 3, TE. Assign the activity in the caption. **(BASIC)**
- ❑ **Express Lesson** Evaluating Healthcare Products, SE. Have students complete this lesson to learn how to evaluate healthcare products.
- ❑ **Life Skills Worksheet** Express Lesson: Evaluating Healthcare Products, CRF. Have students use this worksheet to help them evaluate OTC medicines. **(GENERAL)**
- ❑ **Express Lesson** Responding to a Medical Emergency, SE. Have students complete this lesson to learn how to respond to medical emergencies.
- ❑ **Life Skills Worksheet** Express Lesson: Responding to a Medical Emergency, CRF. Have students use this worksheet to learn about medical emergencies. **(GENERAL)**

CLOSE *10 minutes*

- ❑ **Concept Review Worksheet** Section 2, CRF. This exercise reinforces the material covered in the section. **(GENERAL)**
- ❑ **Section Quiz** Section 2, CRF. Students answer five questions that review the section content. **(GENERAL)**

HOMEWORK *30 minutes*

- ❑ **Life Skills Worksheet** Comparing OTC Medicines, CRF. Students evaluate media messages about OTC medications. **(GENERAL)**
- ❑ **Decision-Making Activity** Using Legal Drugs Safely, CRF. Students create public service announcements on safe drug use. **(GENERAL)**
- ❑ **Section Review** Section 2, SE. Assign questions 1–10 for review, homework, or as a quiz.

OTHER RESOURCE OPTIONS

- ❑ **Reteaching Worksheet** Section 2, CRF. Students complete this worksheet to reinforce the ideas of the section. **(BASIC)**

Lesson Plan *continued*

- ❑ **Datasheet for Analyzing Data** Reading a Prescription Label, CRF. Students answer questions about proper use of a medication based on the label. **(GENERAL)**
- ❑ **Group Activity** OTC Debate, TE. Have students debate whether the FDA should make more drugs available over the counter. **(ADVANCED)**
- ❑ **Life Skill Builder** Making Responsible Decisions, TE. Have students research the difference between a generic and a brand name OTC medication. **(ADVANCED)**
- ❑ **Reading Skill Builder** Active Reading, TE. Ask students to write a mock e-mail to a friend giving advice about treating a health problem. **(BASIC)**
- ❑ **Express Lesson** Selecting Healthcare Services, SE. Have students complete this lesson to learn how to select a healthcare provider.
- ❑ **Life Skills Worksheet** Express Lesson: Selecting Healthcare Services, CRF. Students follow the steps to choose a qualified healthcare provider. **(BASIC)**
- ❑ **Express Lesson** Financing Your Health Care, SE. Have students complete this lesson to learn about health insurance plans.
- ❑ **Life Skills Worksheet** Express Lesson: Financing Your Healthcare, CRF. Students compare health insurance plans and HMOs/PPOs. **(BASIC)**
- ❑ **Activity** Talking to a Pharmacist, TE. Have students role-play a conversation between a patient who has a drug sensitivity and a pharmacist. **(GENERAL)**
- ❑ **Activity** Pharmacists' Training, TE. Have students research and report on the educational requirements for pharmacists. **(GENERAL)**
- ❑ **Using the Figure** Figure 4, TE. Assign the activity in the caption. **(BASIC)**
- ❑ **Internet Connect** Medicine Safety, HealthLinks code: HH4096. Students use Internet sources to research medicine safety.
- ❑ **Internet Connect** Drug Interactions, HealthLinks code: HH4049. Students use Internet sources to research drug interactions.
- ❑ **Internet Connect** Drug-Food Reactions, HealthLinks code: HH4052. Students use Internet sources to research drug-food reactions.
- ❑ **Guided Reading Audio CD Program** Understanding Drugs and Medicines Script. Assign Section 2. The audio program is a reading of the chapter content for ELL students, auditory learners, and struggling readers.

Lesson Plan

Section: Drugs and the Brain

Pacing

1 block = 45 minutes

Regular Schedule	**with lab(s):** N/A	**without lab(s):** 1 day
Block Schedule	**with lab(s):** N/A	**without lab(s):** 0.5 day

Objectives

1. Describe how drugs that affect the brain work.
2. State how drugs can affect a person's emotions.
3. Describe how addiction can develop from experimentation.
4. Summarize the role of withdrawal in maintaining a drug addiction.
5. Describe why addiction is considered a treatable and avoidable disease.

National Health Education Standards Covered

1.1 Analyze how behavior can impact health maintenance and disease prevention.

1.3 Explain the impact of personal health behaviors on the functioning of body systems.

1.6 Describe how to delay onset and reduce risks of potential health problems during adulthood.

2.4 Demonstrate the ability to access school and community health services for self and others.

2.6 Analyze situations requiring professional health services.

3.3 Analyze the short-term and long-term consequences of safe, risky, and harmful behaviors.

3.5 Develop injury prevention and management strategies for personal, family, and community health.

4.3 Evaluate the impact of technology on personal, family, and community health.

5.1 Demonstrate skills for communicating effectively with family, peers, and others.

5.3 Demonstrate healthy ways to express needs, wants, and feelings.

6.3 Predict immediate and long-term impact of health decisions on the individual, family, and community.

7.2 Express information and opinions about health issues.

7.4 Demonstrate the ability to influence and support others in making positive health choices.

Lesson Plan *continued*

KEY
SE = Student Edition
TE = Teacher Edition
CRF = Chapter Resource File

Block 3

FOCUS *5 minutes*

- ❑ **Bellringer** TE. Have students respond to the statement, "If I want to use drugs, it's my choice and it doesn't affect anyone else besides me." **(GENERAL)**

MOTIVATE *5 minutes*

- ❑ **Activity** Drugs and Violence, TE. Ask students to discuss examples of crime or violence as a result of drug abuse and list the victims involved. **(GENERAL)**

TEACH *20 minutes*

- ❑ **Express Lesson** Nervous System, SE. Have students complete this lesson to learn more about the nervous system.
- ❑ **Life Skills Worksheet** Express Lesson: Nervous System, CRF. Have students write a travel brochure that serves as a guide to the nervous system. **(ADVANCED)**
- ❑ **Group Activity** Drug Addiction, TE. Have students work in groups to role-play a group of friends in which one member has a drug addiction. **(GENERAL)**
- ❑ **Express Lesson** Public Health, SE. Have students complete this lesson to learn more about public health issues.
- ❑ **Life Skills Worksheet** Express Lesson: Public Health, CRF. Have students use this worksheet to help them understand public health. **(GENERAL)**
- ❑ **Datasheet for In-Text Activity** Making GREAT Decisions, CRF. Use the GREAT decision-making steps to write down a plan to confront a friend about drug abuse. **(GENERAL)**
- ❑ **Teaching Transparency** Nerve Cell. Use this graphic when teaching the students about the effects of drugs on the body.

CLOSE *15 minutes*

- ❑ **Concept Review Worksheet** Section 3, CRF. This exercise reinforces the material covered in the section. **(GENERAL)**
- ❑ **Section Quiz** Section 3, CRF. Students answer five questions that review the lesson content. **(GENERAL)**

HOMEWORK *30 minutes*

- ❑ **Section Review** Section 3, SE. Assign questions 1–10 for review, homework, or as a quiz.
- ❑ **Chapter Review** Understanding Drugs and Medicines, SE. Assign questions to review the material for this chapter.

OTHER RESOURCE OPTIONS

- ❑ **Reteaching Worksheet** Section 3, CRF. Students complete this worksheet to reinforce the ideas of the section. **(BASIC)**
- ❑ **Reading Skill Builder** Healthy Vocabulary. Ask students the difference between psychological and physiological dependency. **(GENERAL)**
- ❑ **Activity** Illegal Drugs in the Community, TE. Students research and discuss the use of illegal drugs in their community. **(GENERAL)**
- ❑ **Life Skills Worksheet** Writing a Public Service Announcement, CRF. Students plan and design a PSA about effects of drug use on the brain. **(BASIC)**
- ❑ **Decision-Making Activity** Health Careers, CRF. Students learn more about health careers. **(GENERAL)**
- ❑ **Internet Connect** Medicines from Plants, HealthLinks code: HH4097. Students use Internet sources to research medicines from plants.
- ❑ **Internet Connect** Nervous System, HealthLinks code: HH4105. Students use Internet sources to research drug and alcohol abuse.
- ❑ **Guided Reading Audio CD Program** Understanding Drugs and Medicines Script. Assign Section 3. The audio program is a reading of the chapter content for ELL students, auditory learners, and struggling readers.

Block 4

END-OF-CHAPTER ASSESSMENT *45 minutes*

- ❑ **Chapter Test** Understanding Drugs and Medicines, CRF. Assign questions for general level chapter assessment. **(GENERAL)**
- ❑ **Chapter Test** Understanding Drugs and Medicines, CRF. Assign questions for advanced level chapter assessment. **(ADVANCED)**

ALTERNATIVE ASSESSMENT *45 minutes*

- ❑ **Alternative Assessment** Understanding Drugs and Medicines, CRF. Assign questions for general level chapter assessment. **(GENERAL)**
- ❑ **Standardized Test Practice** Understanding Drugs and Medicines, CRF. Students answer questions to help them prepare for standardized tests. **(GENERAL)**
- ❑ **Test Item Listing** Understanding Drugs and Medicines, CRF. Create a customized homework assignment, quiz, or test using the HRW Test Generator program.

Parent Discussion Guide

Parent Letter

Dear Parent/Guardian,

In the next few weeks, your teen's Health Education class will focus on the use, misuse, and abuse of medicines and drugs.

We live in a drug-oriented society. We are surrounded by advertisements that suggest that if we feel pain, all we have to do is take a medicine. In this chapter, your teen will learn about using medicines wisely and safely. Students will also study the various categories of medicines. We will discuss the difference between over-the-counter and prescription medications and the importance of understanding how different medicines can interact.

You can actively support your teen's progress in Lifetime Health by communicating with him or her about the topics covered in this course. To aid this communication, I have included a Parental Survey worksheet for you to complete with your teen. Your signature at the end of this material will verify that this home interaction has taken place.

Thank you in advance for your time, cooperation, and support.

Sincerely,

____

Health Teacher

Parent Discussion Guide

Parental Survey

Complete the following survey together.

There are differences in the definitions of drug use, drug misuse, and drug abuse. To make sure you understand their differences, review the definitions in the chapter together. Next, read each statement or scenario and together try to decide if what you read is an example of drug use (DU), drug misuse (DM), or drug abuse (DA). The correct answers are below.

______ **1.** Cindi smokes a little marijuana before her classes each day.

______ **2.** Tom takes his father's prescription medicine for his stomach pain.

______ **3.** Jose uses his own inhaler for his asthmatic condition.

______ **4.** Tamika takes three pain tablets instead of the recommended two because her headache is worse this time.

______ **5.** Because he was feeling better, Myron stopped taking his antibiotics two days before he was supposed to stop.

______ **6.** Anita's mother takes the prescribed dosage of cough syrup for her cough.

______ **7.** Alan, Linda, and Neil all get together to smoke a cigarette before school starts each day.

______ **8.** Artisha, Chris, and Nicole always go out drinking before their Friday night high school football game.

ANSWERS—**1.** DA **2.** DM **3.** DU **4.** DM **5.** DM **6.** DU **7.** DA **8.** DA

The signatures below verify that our discussion has taken place.

______________________________ ______________

Student Signature Class Period

______________________________ ______________

Signature of Parent or Guardian Date

Answer Key

Life Skills

COMPARING MEDICINE PRICES

1. The packaging for the brand-name drug is much more stylized and flashy than the packaging of the generic brand.
2. Students will probably suggest that the brand-name package has more appeal and is easier to recognize because the design is eye-catching and distinctive.
3. Students may suggest that manufacturers choose stylized packaging so that their products attract attention and are easily recognizable.
4. The store-brand drug costs $2.48 less than the brand-name drug. Students may suggest that fancy packaging costs more or that people are willing to pay more for name recognition. Some students may observe that the amount of drug in each tablet is not available on either container. The difference in cost may reflect a difference in the size or potency of a tablet.
5. A brand-name drug is made by the company that developed the drug. A generic drug is made by a company other than the one that developed the drug.
6. Students may suggest reading the ingredients on the label of each drug or asking a pharmacist.

COMPARING OVER-THE-COUNTER MEDICINES

1. The characteristics of the OTC medicines will vary depending upon the individual medicines.
2. Three possible guidelines for choosing an OTC medicine are as follows: Decide what kind of OTC medicine will work for you. Decide whether you want a generic or a brand-name medicine. Read the label for directions and warnings.
3. Answers may vary. An ad for an OTC medicine allows one to follow safety guidelines by providing ingredients, uses, warnings of possible side effects, directions for correct dosage, and directions for frequency of doses.
4. Answers may vary depending on how well the chosen ad addresses the guidelines for choosing an OTC medicine.

WRITING A PUBLIC SERVICE ANNOUNCEMENT

1. Answers may vary, but students should select a positive-consequence message, a negative-consequence message, or a message conveying refusal strategies.
2. Students' messages may vary, but they should convey how drugs affect the brain. Students may use positive-consequence messages to emphasize the positive outcome of using drugs safely, negative-consequence messages to emphasize the harmful effects of drug misuse or abuse, or messages about refusal strategies.
3. Answers may vary.
4. PSAs may vary. Accept scripts, posters, essays, and so on that convey the consequences of drug misuse or abuse in a way that is sensitive to the intended audience.

Express Lesson

EVALUATING HEALTHCARE PRODUCTS

1. The advertisement claims that the supplement treats both obesity and fatigue. It promises fast results and describes the supplement as a miracle. The product is available only through the mail, through a post-office box. The supplement is claimed to be a scientific breakthrough overlooked by the medical community.
2. Ephedra and Ma huang are different names for the same drug. This substance has been linked to several deaths, as well as to stroke, heart attack, and psychotic episodes in previously healthy young individuals. Its effects are magnified by caffeine. Ginger has no proven effect on weight

loss or metabolism. Extensive peer-reviewed research has shown that chromium picolinate does not play a role in weight loss, although it can help regulate blood glucose in a small proportion of diabetics. Cayenne pepper increases metabolism slightly, but not in the proportions present in the supplement. Willow bark extract is the original source of aspirin. (Early Native Americans chewed it for pain relief.) People with aspirin allergy might experience a life-threatening anaphylactic reaction to this product.

NERVOUS SYSTEM

1. Answers may vary, but they might include the various parts of the brain, the spinal cord, and the sensory and motor nerves.
2. Answers may include sensation (taste, touch, smell, sound, sight), movement, reflexes, and automatic activities such as heartbeat, breathing, digestion, and swallowing.
3. Answers may include messages gathered by the peripheral nervous system from inside and outside the body. These signals are "imported" to the central nervous system, from which they are "exported" as signals back to the muscles and nerves of the body.
4. Students might respond that sensory and motor nerves, if injured, heal very slowly, while spinal nerves do not generally grow well enough to repair significant damage. They might also note that damage to the medulla oblongata can interfere with many automatic activities central to life.
5. Students' brochures should identify the various components of the nervous system and address each question in a creative manner.

SELECTING HEALTHCARE SERVICES

1. Students may differ in their criteria. Some may indicate that, in addition to the qualities listed, having a doctor of the same gender is important.
2. Tables may vary depending on the physicians selected. Students should highlight the doctor(s) that best meet their criteria.

FINANCING YOUR HEALTHCARE

Part I

HMO

Description: A basic type of managed care in which patients must use a doctor who is part of the insurance company's contract.
Benefits: Less expensive than traditional insurance plans.
Drawbacks: Patients have a limited choice of providers.The insurance company will not pay for the services of a provider who is not part of its contract.

PPO

Description: A type of managed care in which the patient has the option to see a doctor who is not on the insurance company's contract.
Benefits: More flexibility in selection of healthcare provider.
Drawbacks: When seeing a doctor who is not part of the insurance company's contract, patients must pay a higher co-payment fee.

Part II

1. Answers may vary. Students should note that if their doctor is not part of the plan, their payment will increase.
2. Most HMOs and PPOs do require that a primary care provider be selected. Many permit women, however, to see any obstetrician-gynecologist in the plan without referral from the PCP. Often, plans provide biographical information about the primary care providers that can help when making a decision.
3. Out-of-plan payments will vary, but exceed the usual payment. Most plans make exceptions in cases of emergency or when the patient is in excess of a specified distance from his or her primary care provider.

Reteaching

SECTION: DRUGS

Part I

1. **a.** relieves pain
   b. acetaminophen
2. **a.** causes sleepiness
   b. temazepam
3. **a.** increases alertness
   b. focuses attention in ADHD patients
   c. methylphenidate

Part II

4. safety and effectiveness
5. Any drug that is used to cure, prevent, or treat illness or discomfort is a medicine. A drug of abuse has mind-altering effects and no medical purpose.

SECTION: DRUGS AS MEDICINES

1. acetaminophen
2. headache, backache, muscular aches, toothache, aches from the common cold, arthritic pain, and fever
3. 2 tablets every 4 to 6 hours, not to exceed 8 tablets in 24 hours
4. Acetaminophen can cause liver damage.

SECTION: DRUGS AND THE BRAIN

Part I

1. addicted
2. behavior
3. drug use
4. psychoactive
5. withdrawal
6. tolerance
7. physical
8. alcohol

Part II

9. loss of interest in schoolwork
10. dramatic change of appearance
11. change of friends
12. unexplained mood swings

Concept Review

SECTION: DRUGS

Part I

1. a
2. c
3. d

Part II

4. safety, effectiveness, mild side effects
5. A drug is any substance that causes a change in a person's physical or psychological state, while a medicine is a drug used to cure, prevent, or treat illness or discomfort.
6. Drugs of abuse are taken for mind-altering effects rather than for a medical purpose.

SECTION: DRUGS AS MEDICINES

Part I

1. Prescription medicines are often powerful and often treat serious illnesses.
2. dose, timing, frequency, and duration
3. cell culture testing, animal testing, testing on healthy human subjects, clinical trials

Part II

4. c
5. d
6. d
7. a

SECTION: DRUGS AND THE BRAIN

Part I

1. withdrawal
2. neurotransmitters
3. physical dependence
4. addiction
5. tolerance

Part II

6. a
7. b
8. d
9. c

Quiz

SECTION: DRUGS

1. d
2. a
3. e
4. b
5. c

SECTION: DRUGS AS MEDICINES

Part I

1. c
2. b
3. a

Part II

4. c
5. b

SECTION: DRUGS AND THE BRAIN

1. d
2. b
3. d
4. a
5. a

Chapter Test General

Part I

1. c
2. d
3. f
4. b
5. a
6. h
7. g
8. e

Part II

9. a
10. d
11. b
12. d
13. b
14. d
15. c
16. d
17. d
18. a
19. b
20. d

Chapter Test Advanced

Part I

1. a
2. c
3. b
4. d

Part II

5. b
6. a
7. c
8. d
9. b
10. d

Part III

11. f
12. i
13. d
14. a
15. e
16. b
17. g
18. c
19. h

Part IV

20. Answers may vary, but they should reflect the understanding that dopamine is a neurotransmitter that produces pleasure. When people experiment with drugs of abuse, pleasure reinforces the drug use. Experimentation can progress to a more established pattern of use, then to tolerance, dependence, and addiction. Addiction is treatable, but the best way to avoid it is to avoid drugs.

Alternative Assessment

Presentations may vary, but should demonstrate a thorough understanding of the topic chosen. Encourage students to be as creative and informative as possible. Sketches or summaries should be thorough and easy to understand.

Standardized Test Practice

1. Skill Tested: Forming an Analogy
A Incorrect. Aspirin is another type of over-the-counter medicine.
B Incorrect. Analgesic is a category of medicine.
C Incorrect. Acetaminophen is another type of over-the-counter medicine.
D Correct. Codeine is a specific type of prescription medicine as ibuprofen is a specific type of over-the-counter medicine.

2. Skill Tested: Forming an Analogy
A Correct. Antacids are medicines used to treat heartburn as antihistamines are medicines used to treat the symptoms of allergic reactions.
B Incorrect. Pain is not a symptom treated with antacids. Analgesics treat pain.
C Incorrect. Aspirin is a type of medication, not a symptom treated with medication.
D Incorrect. Histamine is a chemical produced by the body, not a symptom treated with medication.

3. Skill Tested: Applying Knowledge
Responses should show that students realize the danger associated with taking prescription medication prescribed for someone else. Instead, the headache sufferer should take an over-the-counter analgesic.

4. Skill Tested: Identifying the Main Idea
A Incorrect. The passage does not refer to physicians studying new drugs.
B Correct. The main idea of the passage is that all new drugs must go through a rigorous testing process before being approved by the FDA.
C Incorrect. Animal testing is only one step in the FDA's approval process.
D Incorrect. While choice B is correct, choice A is incorrect.

5. Skill Tested: Identifying Supporting Details
   - **A** Incorrect. Both choices A and B occur during clinical trials.
   - **B** Incorrect. Both choices A and B occur during clinical trials.
   - **C** Incorrect. Laboratory testing of a new drug occurs before clinical trials.
   - **D** Correct. The passage states that during clinical trials a new drug is given to humans who have the illness it is meant to treat and compared to existing drugs.
6. Skill Tested: Sequencing Events
   Responses should note the following sequence of events: new drug is discovered, tested in laboratories, tested on animals, tested on healthy human volunteers, tested on humans who have the illness the drug is meant to treat, compared to existing drugs for safety and effectiveness, approved by the FDA.
7. Skill Tested: Cause and Effect Relationships
   - **A** Incorrect. The passage does not suggest that these drugs trigger such feelings in the user.
   - **B** Incorrect. The passage states that the user may become physically addicted to these drugs, not physically ill from them.
   - **C** Correct. The passage explains that since these drugs interrupt the balance between the neurotransmitters in the user's brain, the individual's judgement is impaired.
   - **D** Incorrect. Neither choice A or B is correct.
8. Skill Tested: Cause and Effect Relationships
   - **A** Incorrect. Both A and B are correct.
   - **B** Incorrect. Both A and B are correct.
   - **C** Incorrect. While a person may use a drug as a means of escaping reality, addiction is not an inability to deal with reality.
   - **D** Correct. The passage notes that a person who is addicted to a drug cannot function without it and has a physical need for the substance.
9. Skill Tested: Applying Knowledge
   Responses may vary. Students who do choose to discuss the situation should support their position with a description of how the drug affects the functioning of the user's brain.
10. Skill Tested: Interpreting Graphs
    - **A** Correct. About 0.9 million people misuse stimulants while roughly 1.4 million people misuse antianxiety medication. 1.4 – 0.9 = 0.5
    - **B** Incorrect. The difference between 1.4 and 0.9 is 0.5, not 1.
    - **C** Incorrect. The difference between 1.4 and 0.9 is 0.5, not 1.5
    - **D** Incorrect. The difference between 1.4 and 0.9 is 0.5, not 5.
11. Skill Tested: Equivalent Ratios
    - **A** Correct. About 0.9 million people misuse stimulants while roughly 2.7 million people misuse pain relievers. 0.9 : 2.7 reduces to 1 : 3.
    - **B** Incorrect. 0.9 : 2.7 reduces to 1 : 3, not 1 : 5.
    - **C** Incorrect. 0.9 : 2.7 reduces to 1 : 3, not 2 : 5.
    - **D** Incorrect. This ratio compares the number of people who misuse pain relievers to those who misuse stimulants. It should be reversed.
12. Skill Tested: Applying Concepts
    Students should explain to the family member that the pharmacist is actually doing his job by not refilling the prescription without authorization from a physician. His actions will prevent the family member from misusing or even becoming addicted to the medication.

Datasheet for In-Text Activity

ANALYZING DATA: READING A PRESCRIPTION LABEL

1. three times a day
2. yes
3. drowsiness
4. 30 days
5. It is best for Zola to contact her doctor before she stops taking her medication.

MAKING GREAT DECISIONS

Answers may vary. Sample answer: I can ask Dave to come over and shoot hoops. Before he comes, I should plan what I want to say to Dave. If he does not come over, I should assure Dave that we are still friends and if he feels like talking sometime, I am available. I should also consider talking to a trusted adult about my concerns.

Decision-Making Activity

REASONS FOR USE OF LEGAL DRUGS

1. Answers may include any situation in which OTC drugs are used to treat common illnesses, injuries, or disorders. For example, headaches can be treated with acetaminophen, allergies can be treated with diphenhydramine, a skin rash can be treated with cortisone, and a stuffy nose can be treated with pseudoephedrine.
2. acetaminophen (pain relief), diphenhydramine (antihistamine), aluminum hydroxide (antacid), cortisone cream (steroid anti-inflammatory), and so on
3. Answers may vary, but they might include making sure that the medicine taken is appropriate for the illness/condition to be treated; reading the label and following directions; being alert to side effects and discontinuing the medication if side effects occur; and seeking the advice of a doctor if symptoms worsen or do not improve. Students should also include guidelines that help identify whether lifestyle changes might improve the condition, making the use of OTC medications unnecessary. For example, chronic stress can cause headaches, and learning relaxation techniques might help avoid the need for prolonged or repeated use of acetaminophen or ibuprofen.
4. Presentations may vary, but they should include a complete set of guidelines for the use of OTC medications, as well as guidelines designed to help avoid the need for prolonged or repeated use.

USING LEGAL DRUGS SAFELY

1–3. Students' public service announcements (PSAs) may vary according to the guideline chosen. However, they should reflect the understanding that the issues presented in PSAs often trigger strong emotions or opinions in the audience, and the PSAs should be written with this in mind. In addition, each message should be appropriately geared to the high school audience. Upon choosing the issue to address, groups should use library or Internet resources to gather the most up-to-date information possible. (For example, a PSA that presents the directive to keep all drugs away from children might include statistics about the number of emergency room visits or deaths that are attributable to accidental poisoning of children by OTC and prescription medications.) Groups should then write a convincing announcement that thoroughly addresses the guideline they chose to present.

TEST ITEM LISTING

Understanding Drugs and Medicines

MATCHING

a. medicine
b. drug interaction
c. allergic reaction
d. drug use
e. serotonin
f. side effect
g. dose, frequency, timing, and duration
h. stimulant
i. psychoactive drug
j. safety, effectiveness, and minor side effects
k. addiction
l. anaphylactic shock
m. drug
n. generic medicine
o. prescription
p. avoidable and treatable

1. ____ a medicine made by a company other than the company that developed the original medicine
Answer: n Difficulty: 1 Section: 2 Objective: 3

2. ____ a life-threatening reaction to a drug
Answer: l Difficulty: 1 Section: 1 Objective: 3

3. ____ a substance that causes a change in a person's physical or psychological state
Answer: m Difficulty: 1 Section: 1 Objective: 1

4. ____ a doctor's written order for a specific medicine
Answer: o Difficulty: 1 Section: 2 Objective: 3

5. ____ qualities possessed by a medicine
Answer: j Difficulty: 1 Section: 1 Objective: 1

6. ____categories that drug addiction falls into
Answer: p Difficulty: 1 Section: 3 Objective: 3

7. ____a condition in which a person can no longer control his or her drug use
Answer: k Difficulty: 1 Section: 3 Objective: 3

8. ____taking a medicine exactly as directed
Answer: d Difficulty: 1 Section: 2 Objective: 5

9. ____a change in the effect of a drug that occurs as a result of it being taken with another drug
Answer: b Difficulty: 1 Section: 2 Objective: 4

10. ____ a potentially serious side effect of a medicine
Answer: c Difficulty: 1 Section: 2 Objective: 4

11. ____ any drug used to cure, prevent, or treat illness or discomfort
Answer: a Difficulty: 1 Section: 1 Objective: 1

12. ____a drug that speeds up body functions
Answer: h Difficulty: 1 Section: 1 Objective: 3

13. ____ information included in a prescription
Answer: g Difficulty: 1 Section: 2 Objective: 2

14. ____a neurotransmitter that brings about feelings of pleasure
Answer: e Difficulty: 1 Section: 3 Objective: 2

15. ____ an effect that is caused by a drug and is different from the drug's intended effect
Answer: f Difficulty: 1 Section: 2 Objective: 4

16 ____ a drug or medicine that affects thoughts, perceptions, or feelings
Answer: i Difficulty: 1 Section: 2 Objective: 2

MULTIPLE CHOICE

17. The brain reward system describes how
   a. drugs of abuse are taken into the body.
   b. neurotransmitters release chemicals at synapses.
   c. the release of dopamine causes pleasure, reinforcing a behavior.
   d. students can get good grades by studying hard.

   Answer: c Difficulty: 1 Section: 3 Objective: 3

18. Drugs can enter your body
   a. through inhalation and ingestion.
   b. by release from implanted pumps or injection.
   c. via transdermal patches and topical application.
   d. All of the above

   Answer: d Difficulty: 1 Section: 1 Objective: 4

19. The agency responsible for ensuring the safety of food, drugs, and cosmetics is
   a. the Food and Drug Administration.
   b. the Department of Health and Human Services.
   c. the Department of the Interior.
   d. the Office of the Surgeon General of the United States.

   Answer: a Difficulty: 1 Section: 2 Objective: 1

20. Peter broke his arm playing football. The doctor wrote a prescription for a painkiller. The prescription said to take one tablet every four hours as needed for pain. Peter only took two tablets—one after he got home from having his arm set and another 4 hours later. Those were the only times his arm hurt. Peter
   a. abused the painkillers.
   b. used the painkillers correctly.
   c. misused the painkillers.
   d. became addicted to the painkillers.

   Answer: b Difficulty: 1 Section: 2 Objective: 5

21. Steve is suffering from a headache and congestion. When choosing an over-the-counter (OTC) medicine, he should
   a. read labels to see which medicine will best relieve his symptoms.
   b. choose a generic drug.
   c. choose a brand-name drug.
   d. choose an antihistamine.

   Answer: a Difficulty: 1 Section: 2 Objective: 3

22. Herbal remedies and dietary supplements differ from OTC medicines because
   a. they are not regulated by the FDA in the same way OTC medicines are.
   b. they do not work.
   c. they are safer than medicines.
   d. they are more thoroughly researched.

   Answer: a Difficulty: 1 Section: 2 Objective: 1

23. Prescriptions are required for some drugs because
   a. some illnesses are serious and should be evaluated by a doctor.
   b. some prescription medicines are very powerful.
   c. prescriptions require that a doctor evaluate your needs.
   d. All of the above

   Answer: d Difficulty: 1 Section: 2 Objective: 2

24. The effects of a medicine can be influenced by whether
    a. it was taken with a lot of water.
    b. it was taken with another medicine.
    c. it was sold over the counter.
    d. it was in a safety bottle.

    Answer: b Difficulty: 1 Section: 2 Objective: 4

25. Dewayne had a bad cold. He decided to take an over-the-counter medication to help relieve his cold symptoms. After he took the medication he began to feel very sleepy. This feeling of sleepiness is most likely due to
    a. side effects of the drug.
    b. misuse of the drug.
    c. interactions among drugs.
    d. an allergy.

    Answer: a Difficulty: 1 Section: 2 Objective: 4

26. Which of the following is *not* an over-the-counter drug?
    a. ibuprofen
    b. antibiotic
    c. antihistamine
    d. cortisone cream

    Answer: b Difficulty: 1 Section: 1 Objective: 3

27. Problems that can occur as a result of drug use include
    a. allergic reactions.
    b. side effects.
    c. drug interactions.
    d. All of the above

    Answer: d Difficulty: 1 Section: 2 Objective: 4

28. Which of the following is *not* found on a prescription label?
    a. possible side effects of the drug
    b. refill information
    c. dose information
    d. the amount of the drug in the prescription

    Answer: a Difficulty: 1 Section: 2 Objective: 2

29. Carla's doctor prescribed an antibiotic for her sinus infection. After taking the medicine, her skin became itchy, and she started to wheeze. Which statement describes Carla's situation?
    a. She might be experiencing an anaphylactic reaction to the antibiotic.
    b. She might be experiencing a life-threatening reaction.
    c. She might require emergency medical care.
    d. all of the above

    Answer: d Difficulty: 1 Section: 2 Objective: 4

30. The path to addiction follows which of the following sequences?
    a. drug use, dependence, tolerance, addiction
    b. dependence, tolerance, drug use, addiction
    c. drug use, tolerance, dependence, addiction
    d. drug use, dependence, addiction, tolerance

    Answer: c Difficulty: 1 Section: 3 Objective: 3

31. What is the sequence of events in the approval of a medicine for human use?
    a. laboratory testing (chemical or cell), animal testing, testing on healthy humans, clinical trials
    b. animal testing, testing on cell cultures, testing on healthy humans, clinical trials
    c. laboratory testing (chemical or cell), animal testing, clinical trials, testing on healthy humans
    d. animal testing, laboratory testing (chemical or cell), clinical trials, testing on healthy humans

    Answer: a Difficulty: 1 Section: 2 Objective: 1

32. If you are feeling depressed or anxious about something, what should you do first to try to solve your problem?
    a. Take a couple of aspirin and read a book.
    b. Go out and have fun drinking beer with your friends.
    c. Talk over your problems with someone you trust.
    d. Get a mild tranquilizer from your doctor.

    Answer: c   Difficulty: 1   Section: 2   Objective: 5

COMPLETION

33. Analgesics are used to ____________________.
    Answer: relieve pain   Difficulty: 2   Section: 1   Objective: 3

34. A medicine that increases alertness and helps a person with ADHD focus his or her attention is called a(n) ____________________.
    Answer: stimulant   Difficulty: 2   Section: 1   Objective: 3

35. Amoxicillin is a(n) ____________________, which acts by killing bacteria to help cure infections.
    Answer: antibiotic   Difficulty: 2   Section: 1   Objective: 3

36. A ____________________ is a prescription drug that might be useful to treat insomnia.
    Answer: sedative   Difficulty: 2   Section: 1   Objective: 3

37. Itchy skin might be relieved by the topical application of a(n) ____________________, such as cortisone cream.
    Answer: steroid anti-inflammatory
    Difficulty: 2   Section: 1   Objective: 3

38. A condition in which the body relies on a given drug to help it function is ____________________.
    Answer: physical dependence
    Difficulty: 2   Section: 3   Objective: 3

39. Insulin is a(n) ____________________ that lowers blood sugar.
    Answer: hormone   Difficulty: 2   Section: 1   Objective: 3

40. Applying medicine directly to certain body areas for absorption through the skin is called ____________________.
    Answer: topical application
    Difficulty: 2   Section: 1   Objective: 4

41. Three problems that can occur when you take a medicine are ____________________.
    Answer: drug allergies, side effects, and drug interactions
    Difficulty: 2   Section: 2   Objective: 4

42. When choosing an OTC medication, two factors to consider are ____________________.
    Answer:
    the kind of OTC medication that will work best for you and whether you want a generic or brand-name medicine
    Difficulty: 2   Section: 2   Objective: 3

43. A substance that is used to cure or treat an illness or injury is called a ____________________.
    Answer: medicine   Difficulty: 2   Section: 1   Objective: 1

44. A drug that increases alertness, such as methylphenidate, is called a(n) ____________________.
    Answer: stimulant   Difficulty: 2   Section: 1   Objective: 3

45. The exact amount of a drug to be taken, specified by a prescription or OTC label, is called its ____________________
Answer: dose Difficulty: 2 Section: 2 Objective: 2

46. A ____________________ drug is a drug or medicine that affects the brain and changes perceptions, thoughts, or feelings.
Answer: psychoactive
Difficulty: 2 Section: 2 Objective: 2

47. An effect that sometimes occurs along with the expected effect of a drug is a ____________________.
Answer: side effect Difficulty: 2 Section: 2 Objective: 4

48. The small spaces between neurons where neurotransmitters are released are called ____________________.
Answer: synapses Difficulty: 2 Section: 3 Objective: 1

SHORT ANSWER

49. Advertisements suggest that drugs make you feel better. How can this be a negative message?
Answer: It might lead people to think that drugs can solve all their problems.
Difficulty: 3 Section: 3 Objective: 3

50. Why are some drugs considered drugs of abuse?
Answer:
because they are taken for their mind-altering effects and have no medical purpose
Difficulty: 3 Section: 1 Objective: 5

51. What type of OTC medicine is acetaminophen? weight-loss pill? cortisone cream?
Answer: analgesic; stimulant; hormone
Difficulty: 3 Section: 1 Objective: 3

52. If you and a friend have the same illness, should you take each other's prescription medications? Why or why not?
Answer:
No, you should not because you might not have the same illness, or one of you might be allergic to the other's medication. In addition, differences in body size and composition may make the dosage inappropriate.
Difficulty: 3 Section: 2 Objective: 2

53. What are three factors that can influence the effect of a medicine?
Answer: dose, the way the drug is administered, and drug interactions
Difficulty: 3 Section: 1 Objective: 3

54. Paul stops taking his antibiotic when he starts to feel better. Why is this not a good idea?
Answer:
Prescriptions should always be taken as directed. Stopping antibiotics too early can prevent recovery from an infection.
Difficulty: 3 Section: 2 Objective: 5

55. How does withdrawal help keep an addiction active?
Answer:
Unpleasant symptoms drive the drug user to take more of the drug in order to feel better.
Difficulty: 3 Section: 3 Objective: 4

56. Franklin takes only prescription drugs that the doctor prescribes for him. Is this an example of drug use, drug misuse, or drug abuse?
Answer: drug use Difficulty: 3 Section: 2 Objective: 5

Use the prescription label shown below to answer the following questions. Write your answers in the spaces provided.

Home Town Pharmacy 200 Alameda Street
Home Town, CA 619-992-9000

RX 1257362 Dr. Takamura 10/15/93
Refills: 0
Drug Exp: 10/94

Smith. Pamela
Take one tablet 4 times daily for 10 days.
28 Penicillin V TAB 500mg
Best if medication is taken on an empty stomach.

57. When was the prescription filled?
    Answer: 10/15/93 Difficulty: 2 Section: 2 Objective: 2
58. Who is the prescription for?
    Answer: Pamela Smith
    Difficulty: 2 Section: 2 Objective: 2
59. Who wrote the prescription?
    Answer: Dr. Takamura
    Difficulty: 2 Section: 2 Objective: 2
60. Where was the prescription filled?
    Answer: Home Town Pharmacy
    Difficulty: 2 Section: 2 Objective: 2
61. How should the medication be taken?
    Answer:
    one tablet 4 times daily on an empty stomach for 10 days
    Difficulty: 2 Section: 2 Objective: 2
62. What is the name of the medication?
    Answer: penicillin V
    Difficulty: 2 Section: 2 Objective: 2
63. What is the dosage of the medication?
    Answer:
    one 500 mg tablet 4 times daily
    Difficulty: 2 Section: 2 Objective: 2
64. When does the medication expire?
    Answer: 10/94 Difficulty: 2 Section: 2 Objective: 2

ESSAY

65. How are drugs, medicines, and herbal remedies alike? How are they different?

    Answer:

    A drug is any substance that causes changes in a person's physical or psychological state. Medicines are drugs that cure, prevent, or treat illness or discomfort. Herbal remedies may be drugs or medicines, but because they are not regulated by the FDA in the same way OTC medicines are, so their safety and effectiveness are not ensured.

    Difficulty: 3 Section: 2 Objective: 1

66. When a person becomes addicted to a drug, what are the physical consequences?

    Answer:

    The person develops a physical need for the drug and suffers withdrawal symptoms if he or she does not take it. A person will know he or she is addicted because he or she will suffer withdrawal symptoms if he or she tries to stop taking the drug.

    Difficulty: 3 Section: 3 Objective: 3

9997255283 2 3 4 5 6